MAD LIBS
WORKBOOK
SUMMER ACTIVITIES

written by Catherine Nichols

MAD LIBS
An imprint of Penguin Random House LLC, New York

First published in the United States of America by Mad Libs,
an imprint of Penguin Random House LLC, New York, 2022

Mad Libs format and text copyright © 2022 by Penguin Random House LLC

Concept created by Roger Price & Leonard Stern

Cover illustration by Scott Brooks
Interior illustrations by Scott Brooks, Tim Haggerty, Gary Lacoste, Scott MacNeil, and Barbara Schaffer

Visit us online at penguinrandomhouse.com.

Printed in the United States of America

ISBN 9780593225790
1 3 5 7 9 10 8 6 4 2
COMM

Designed by Dinardo Design

WORKBOOK

— INSTRUCTIONS —

MAD LIBS WORKBOOK: SUMMER ACTIVITIES is a game for kids who want to have fun in the summer! It is also a review of the key reading skills for Grade 1. It has both skill practice pages and fun story pages.

RIDICULOUSLY SIMPLE DIRECTIONS:

At the top of each story page, you will find up to four columns of words, each headed by a symbol. Each symbol represents a type of word, such as a noun (naming word) or a verb (action word). The categories and symbols change from story to story. Here's an example:

MAD LIBS WORKBOOK: SUMMER ACTIVITIES is fun to play by yourself, but you can also play it with friends, especially in the summer! To begin, look at the story on the page below. When you come to a blank space in the story, look at the symbol that appears underneath. Then find the same symbol on this page and pick a word that appears below the symbol. Write that word in the blank space, and cross out the word, so you don't use it again. Continue doing this throughout the story until you've filled in all the spaces. Finally, read your story aloud and laugh!

EXAMPLE:

I have a new bike. It is _____ and _____ .

I _____ it to the _____ every day.

⚲	🦋	🐴	🍦
purple	wet	~~float~~	kitchen
rusty	~~fuzzy~~	carry	beach
~~round~~	sticky	spin	~~moon~~

I have a new bike. It is ___**round**___ and ___**fuzzy**___ .

I ___**float**___ it to the ___**moon**___ every day.

QUICK REVIEW

In case you haven't learned about phonics yet, here is a quick review:

There are five **VOWELS**: *a*, *e*, *i*, *o*, and *u*. Each vowel has a short sound and a long sound. The long sound of a vowel says its name. Sometimes the consonants *w* and *y* act as vowels when they are in vowel teams, such as *ow* (snow) and *ay* (play).

All the other letters are called **CONSONANTS**.

In case you haven't learned about parts of speech yet, here is a quick review:

NOUNS

A **NOUN** is the name of a person, place, or thing. *Cake*, *hat*, and *owl* are nouns.

cake

hat

owl

VERBS

A **VERB** is an action word. *Kick*, *jump*, and *laugh* are verbs.

kick

jump

laugh

ADJECTIVES

An **ADJECTIVE** describes a person, place, or thing. *Angry*, *green*, and *dirty* are adjectives.

angry

green

dirty

A Is for Animal

Read each word pair.
Draw a circle around the words with the **short a** sound.
Draw a rectangle around the words with the **long a** sound.

snake   bat

map   ape

skates   lamb

plane   cat

cap   whale

cake   rabbit

Camping Out

🍦	🐶	🌴	🍅
dad	play	grapes	lazy
snake	grab	hats	gray
yak	zap	apples	saggy
snail	whack	plates	rainy

My _____ and I went camping. We packed a tent
🍦

and some _____ _____ . I wanted to
🍅 🌴

_____ a game. But first we had to _____
🐶 🐶

_____ _____ . Then we tried to
🍅 🌴

_____ the _____ . At last
🐶 🌴

we were ready. I threw the _____ .
🌴

My _____ _____
🍅 🍦

tried to _____ them. But they
🐶

splashed into the lake.

Picture This!

A **prefix** is a word part added to the beginning of a word. It changes the meaning of the word.

Underline the **prefix** in each sentence. Then draw a picture about the sentence.

The runner's
shoelace is untied.

Return the book
to the library.

The magician made
the rabbit disappear.

The clown is wearing
mismatched socks.

Unbelievable!

🐋	🌶️	🦔	🦴
looking	zoo	sneaker	penguins
beeping	library	spaceship	aliens
smiling	toilet	potato	trolls
burping	park	goldfish	clowns
waving	circus	pumpkin	books

It was an unbelievable day. I went to the _____ .
🌶️

I was _____ at the _____ . I saw that
🐋 🦴

my _____ was untied. So I bent down to tie it.
🦔

When I looked up, I saw a giant _____ ! Two little
🦔

_____ came out of it. They asked if I knew the way to
🦴

the _____ . I helped them find their way,
🌶️

and they gave me a _____ . It is so
🦔

unusual! It keeps _____ at me.
🐋

9

Crossword Fun

Add **s** to most words to make them plural.
Add **es** when the word ends in **x**, **s**, **ss**, **ch**, or **sh**.

Make each word plural by adding **s** or **es**. Then use the words and picture clues to solve the puzzle.

box____   glass____   sock____   brush____

DOWN

1.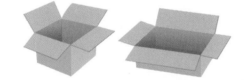

2.

ACROSS

3.

4.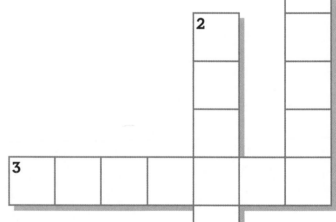

Five Days of Presents

🍕	🦄	👕	🦆
socks	smelly	spiders	neat
balloons	icy	boxes	broken
dishes	big	hugs	skinny
peaches	yucky	splotches	sloppy

On the first day of July,

my grandma sent me _____ _____ .

On the second day of July,

my grandma sent me two _____ _____ .

On the third day of July,

my grandma sent me three _____ _____ .

On the fourth day of July,

my grandma sent me four _____ _____ .

On the fifth day of July, I sent my grandma

five _____ _____ .

Monster Toes

Count each monster's toes. Draw a circle around the monsters with an even number of toes. Draw a rectangle around the monsters with an odd number of toes.

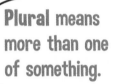

Plural means more than one of something.

Number of toes: _____

Number of toes: _____

Number of toes: _____

Number of toes: _____

Number of toes: _____

Number of toes: _____

Toes is the plural for _____ .

Feet is the plural for _____ .

Find the Words

Words that describe things using our five senses are called **sensory words**. The five senses are **sight**, **sound**, **touch**, **smell**, and **taste**.

Find the 10 sensory words in the word search.

shiny	bumpy	squeaky	smooth	wrinkled
spicy	ringing	salty	buzzing	fishy

B	A	L	L	E	S	H	I	N	Y	R	H
U	U	S	Q	U	E	A	K	Y	D	F	I
M	T	V	W	S	E	L	T	H	B	A	S
P	F	I	S	H	Y	N	T	O	U	L	R
Y	Q	K	Y	T	H	U	O	N	Z	H	I
V	W	R	I	N	K	L	E	D	Z	S	N
S	P	I	C	Y	R	Z	H	R	I	A	G
F	U	O	R	U	F	F	Y	D	N	L	I
A	M	O	K	N	Y	G	E	N	G	T	N
N	D	I	S	M	O	O	T	H	R	Y	G

My Recipe for Ice Cream

🍅	🐟	🐶	🥕
spinach	red	worms	crunchy
milk	chewy	peanuts	hot
salt	slimy	frogs	furry
pizza	sweet	boogers	soft
sugar	fresh	blueberries	salty

Do you like ice cream? I LOVE it! Here is my recipe for

_____ ice cream. Take some _____
🐟   🥕

_____ . Then mix in a cup of _____ .
🍅   🐶

Add some _____ _____ . Then freeze
🐟   🐶

the ice cream and let it get _____ . The
🥕

ice cream is ready when it is _____ .
🥕

Now you can put toppings on the ice cream. Sprinkle

_____ _____ on it. YUM!
🥕   🍅

Animal Matchup

What words have a **short e** sound?
Draw a line from those words to the **hen**.

What words have a **long e** sound?
Draw a line from those words to the **seal**.

seat

cake

bed

hen

we

end

seal

red

pest

key

feet

whale

bread

vine

The Busy Red Hen

🍌	🏀	🌶️	🌴
bread	little	puppy	bake
cheese	lazy	egg	reach
honey	happy	bee	smash
feet	wet	deer	eat
peas	sleepy	troll	peel

Once there was a _____ 🏀 red hen.

The hen wanted to _____ 🌴

some _____ 🍌 . She asked a

_____ 🏀 _____ 🌶️ to help

her. But it said no. Then she asked a _____ 🏀

_____ 🌶️ to help her. But it said no, too. Next she asked

a _____ 🏀 _____ 🌶️ to help her. It also said no.

"All right," said the hen. "I will do it myself." So she did.

Shape Town

Welcome to Shape Town!
How many of these shapes can you find?

Trace the shapes found in the picture.

The word circle
can be both a
noun and a verb.

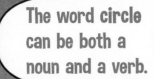

Not a Noun

A **noun** is a naming word.
A person, place, or thing is a noun.

Circle the word in each box that is not a **noun**.

car	bike	slow	cab

park	see	bird	city

seal	clown	circus	funny

eat	cup	plate	spoon

A Strange Dream

🦆	🍦	🐋	🦋
dragon	scary	forest	smiled
troll	little	zoo	burped
unicorn	sweet	cave	stared
elf	green	castle	laughed
frog	huge	car wash	barked

I had a strange dream. I was in a _____ 🍦

_____ 🐋 . A _____ 🍦 _____ 🦆

came by. "Can you help me find my way to the _____ 🐋 ?"

he asked. I took out my map. "Let's go," I said. We walked

and _____ 🦋 . A _____ 🍦

_____ 🦆 appeared. He handed me a

_____ 🍦 _____ 🦆 !

Then I woke up.

Piggy Bank Fun

Write each word on the correct bank.

six	kind	pig	five
pie	fish	dime	pink

Long i Sounds

_____

_____

_____

_____

Short i Sounds

_____

_____

_____

_____

If

🐋	👕	🐶	🌴
pig	little	stick	pie
chin	shiny	fit	wig
fish	gigantic	fry	bib
dime	pink	grill	fig
knight	shy	hide	smile

If you had a _____ _____ , would you
                         👕   🐋

_____ it in a _____ ?
  🐶   🌴

If you had a _____ _____ ,
                      👕   🐋

would you _____ it in a _____ ?
     🐶   🌴

If you had a _____ _____ ,
                      👕   🐋

would you _____ it in a _____ ?
     🐶   🌴

If you had **all** these things, would you _____ them
                            🐶

in a _____ ?
   🌴

Color By Number

Color in each space that equals 5. What do you see?

Tic-Tac-Toe Math

Draw a circle around the three problems with matching answers in each square. Look across, down, and diagonally.

4 − 3	3 + 2	5 + 2
3 + 3	6 − 1	7 − 3
2 + 4	4 + 1	2 + 2

8 + 5	12 − 5	4 + 4
5 − 3	9 − 1	6 + 4
11 − 3	7 − 3	2 + 7

8 − 2	3 − 2	6 + 5
4 + 3	6 + 0	7 − 3
4 + 4	9 + 1	9 − 3

Tough Tongue Twisters

A **verb** is an action word.
Every sentence has a verb.

Circle the verb in each tongue twister.

> She sells seashells by the seashore.

> Bob buys blueberries by the billions.

> Frankie fries fresh fish under the freeway.

> Wally washes windows wearing wide white pants.

> Write your own tongue twister.
>
> _____

Simon Says

🐟	🧁	🦴	🏐
fight	duck	skinny	stick out
tickle	knee	floppy	flap
wiggle	nose	silly	pick
clap	giraffe	broken	stir
draw	tongue	stuffy	touch
lift	shark	tall	sniff

Simon says _____ your _____ _____ .
🏐   🦴   🧁

Simon says _____ your _____ _____ .
🐟   🦴   🧁

Simon   says   _____ your _____ like a
🏐   🧁

_____ _____ .
🦴   🧁

Simon says _____ like a _____ .
🐟   🧁

Simon says _____ your _____
🏐   🧁

around the room. Now _____ !
🐟

Uh-oh! I didn't say Simon says.

A Wet Trip

Add a **verb** to finish each sentence.

jogged   **raced**   **skipped**   **walked**

I _____

around the block.

It started to drizzle,

so I _____ .

Then the rain poured down,

so I _____ home.

I grabbed an umbrella and

_____ to the park.

The Talent Show

🍦	🦆	🥕	🐋
violin	shouted	chuckle	smelly
turnip	whispered	laugh	silly
stage	spoke	crack up	salty
book	screamed	smile	squeaky
tiger	mumbled	giggle	grumpy

I was in a _____ talent show at camp. When it was my turn,
🐋

I stood on the _____ . I took out my _____ .
🍦   🍦

I gave a _____ speech. The people watching began to
🐋

_____ , so I _____ . The people began
🥕   🦆

to _____ , so I _____ .
🥕   🦆

They began to _____ , so I left
🥕

the stage. That's when the _____
🐋

people clapped.

29

Tasty Treats

Count the treats in each group.
Write the numbers in the boxes.
Then write the answer to the problem in the last box.

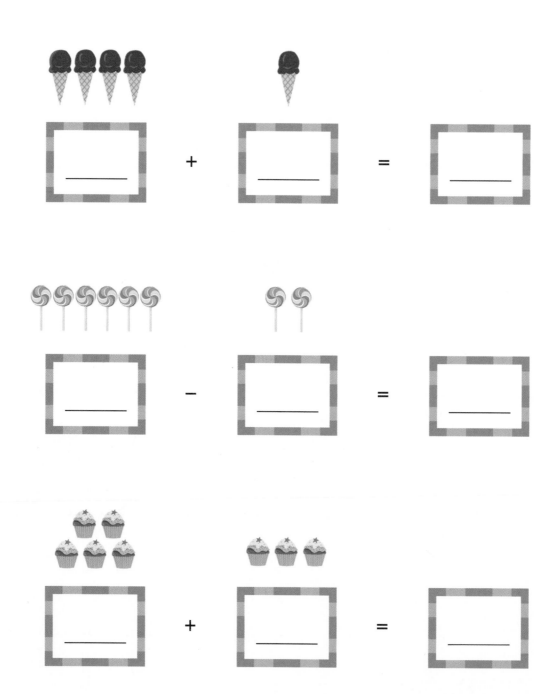

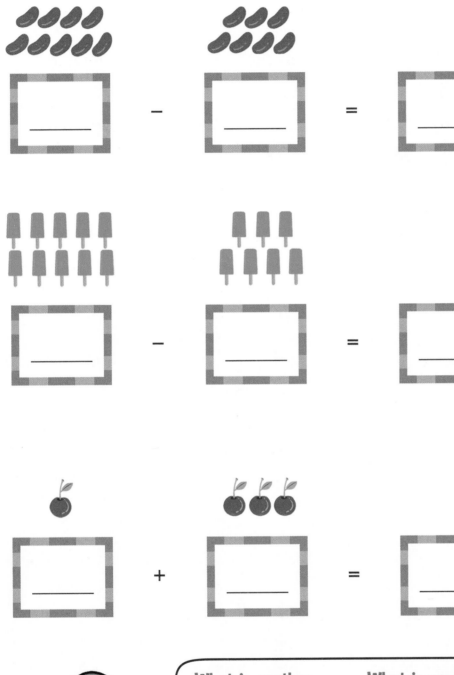

What is another
way to write 3?

What is another
way to write 6?

_____   _____

Word Magic

Presto the Magician can change a cub into a cube.
How? He adds **e**.
Help Presto change the words below. Add **e** to finish each word. Then draw a picture of the new word.

tub____

can____

kit____

not____

My Pet Pete

👕	🍕	🧁	🌶️
mole	skate	game	furry
snake	bite	cave	white
kite	hide	schoolyard	bumpy
dragon	race	bike lane	ripe
mule	sing	nose	huge

My pet Pete is a _____ . Pete is a lot
👕

of fun. He has a _____ tail. He can
🌶️

_____ and _____ . Don't
🍕   🍕

worry. He doesn't _____ . Once I
🍕

put Pete in my _____ backpack and took him to the
🌶️

_____ . But Pete got out! He tried to _____
🧁   🍕

with the _____ . Then he hid in the _____
👕   🌶️

_____ . It was very funny. I love Pete!
🧁

Sort It Out!

This room is a mess! Put the words in the correct category.

ball	kite	pizza
cap	apple	game
sock	shirt	carrot

Clothes Words	Food Words	Toy Words
_____	_____	_____
_____	_____	_____
_____	_____	_____

A New Store

🍌	🦴	🦋	🥕
eggs	blue	beetles	striped
peas	pink	ants	fuzzy
grapes	gray	spiders	moldy
peanuts	yellow	flies	gummy

A new store opened this summer. The food there

is very strange. The _____ are
🍌

_____ and have _____
🦴   🦋

on them. And the _____ are as hard
🍌

as _____ . If you eat one, you could
🦋

break a tooth! If you buy a box of _____ ,
🍌

be careful. Once I found _____ _____
🥕   🦋

inside. The store even has _____ _____ .
🥕   🍌

Yum! I always eat every last one!

Which Way to the Picnic?

An **adjective** is a word that describes something.

The ants are going to a picnic.
Help them get there by following the path of adjectives.

funny

silly

pie

loud

giggle

blue

yummy

bread

jump

hot

dance

fresh

cherry

cheese

chomp

tiny

sunny

Picnic Party

🧁	🍉	🐶	🍦
hungry	cheese	marched	gooey
red	milk	gobbled	sour
smelly	pickles	exploded	yucky
silly	boogers	laughed	yummy
green	cake	burped	sticky

One day a bunch of _____ ants went to a picnic.
🧁

There was a lot of _____ food. The ants ate
🍦

_____ and _____ _____ .
🍉   🍦   🍉

The _____ ants _____ and
🧁   🐶

_____ . They drank _____
🐶   🍦

_____ . Then they _____ .
🍉   🐶

Fill In the Blanks

When two or more consonants are together in a word, they sometimes make a new sound.

Circle the letters to make a word that matches the picture. Then write the letters in the blanks to complete each word.

___ ___ eese

th   ch   sh

ba ___ ___

sh   ch   th

___ ___ ale

wh   sh   th

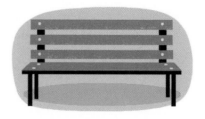

ben ___ ___

ch   th   sh

___ ___ umb

sh   ch   th

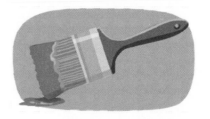

bru ___ ___

th   sh   wh

Very Silly Animal Jokes

🌶️	🌴	🦆	🍅
shark	banana	fetch	whistle
chicken	chair	drink	tooth
whale	road	hug	witch
fish	grass	lick	shoe
sheep	ship	throw	lunch

Why did the _____ _____ the
                          🌶️   🦆

_____ ? **Answer:** To scrub the _____ .
 🍅   🍅

Why did the _____ _____ the
                          🌶️   🦆

_____ ? **Answer:** To eat the _____ .
 🌴   🍅

Why did the _____ _____ the
                          🌶️   🦆

_____ ? **Answer:** To find the _____ .
 🌴   🍅

Laugh It Up!

Add an adjective to finish each sentence.

funny   **hilarious**   **ridiculous**   **clever**

I heard a _____ joke.
It made me think.

I read a _____ book.
I giggled all the way through.

I saw a _____ movie.
I never laughed so hard.

My sister played a _____
prank on me. NOT funny!

The Big Race

👕	🦔	🏀	🍦
snored	highway	slow	speedy
yawned	path	sleepy	fast
burped	iceberg	sluggish	quick
sneezed	banana	lazy	swift

One day a _____ turtle and a _____
🏀   🍦

rabbit had a race. "I will beat you," the rabbit said. "Not so fast,"

said the turtle. "I am _____ , but I may surprise
🏀

you." The rabbit darted ahead. The turtle set off down the

_____ . The rabbit looked back. He couldn't
🦔

see the turtle. The rabbit _____ . "I have plenty of time
👕

for a _____ snooze," he said.
🍦

Who do you think won the race?

41

Fun at the Pool

A **pronoun** takes the place of a noun.

Add a pronoun to finish each sentence.

I	you	her
it	we	me

_____ am going to the pool.

My friend is going with _____ .

She is bringing _____ float.

_____ is big and green.

_____ will have fun!

Do _____ want to come?

My Clever Mom

🥕	🐟	🍍	🐋
mushroom	itchy	scrub	bugs
toilet	sticky	blow	bubbles
dragon	goofy	smell	gerbils
spiderweb	stinky	hear	warts
pickle	furry	tickle	noodles

My mom invents all kinds of _____ things.
🐟

Once she invented a machine for _____ .
🐋

It could _____ your _____ .
🍍   🥕

My dad walked into it. He had _____ all over
🐋

him. He was _____ for a week. But that gave my
🐟

mom a new idea. She invented her best machine ever. My sister and

brother cheered. They were happy. So was I. Now we never have to

_____ the _____ again!
🍍   🥕

Who Can Ride?

These creatures want to go on a ride. Use the tickets to measure each creature and write down your answers. Circle the creature who is tall enough to ride.

Tickets is a plural noun.

YOU MUST BE THIS TALL TO RIDE.

12
11
10
9
8
7
6
5
4
3
2
1

_____ _____ _____ _____

Write three plural nouns from the picture.

_____

_____

_____

Gee, You're Great!

Read each word. If the word starts with a **hard g** sound, like **gorilla**, write the word next to the **gorilla**. If the word starts with a **soft g** sound, like **giraffe**, write the word next to the **giraffe**.

gentle	gym	goat
germ	garden	game

Hard g Words

_____

_____

_____

hmmm?

Soft g Words

_____

_____

_____

The Giant Goldfish

🦴	🍅	🦔	🍕
gorilla	magical	grapes	guess
goose	green	gum	grow
frog	great	gel	hug
slug	huge	ginger	glide
germ	spongy	fudge	giggle

One day a girl named Greta got a goldfish as a gift. She fed the goldfish _____ 🍅 _____ 🦔 . The goldfish gobbled it all up. It grew and grew. Soon it was the size of a _____ 🦴 . It couldn't _____ 🍕 inside its bowl anymore. So the girl gave her goldfish a new home. Now it lives in a pond in the girl's _____ 🦔 . A _____ 🍅 _____ 🦴 lives there, too.

Riddle Me This

What animal wears a coat in the winter and pants in the summer?

Find the answer to the riddle. Color in the lowercase letters in the picture.

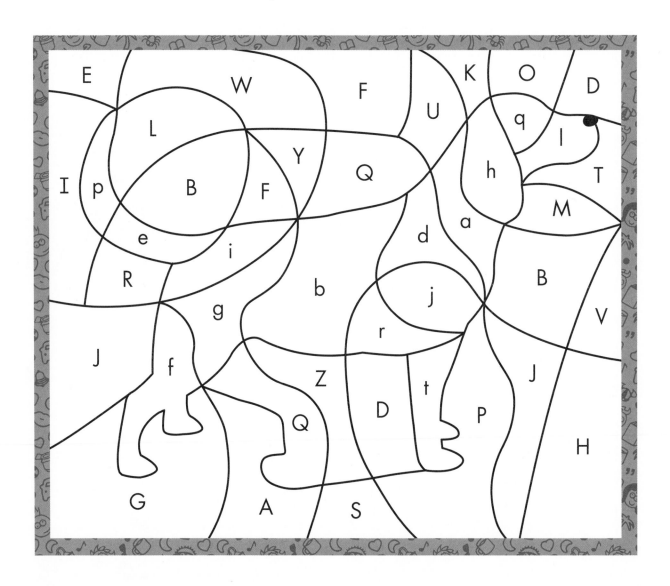

The animal is a _____ .

A Noisy Morning

🐋	🍍	🐶	🥕
motorcycle	smelly	underpants	HONK!
goose	big	teeth	BARK!
lion	loud	worms	RING!
seal	scary	feathers	VROOM!
alarm clock	slimy	earplugs	ROAR!

This morning my _____ (🍍) _____ (🐋) woke

me up. _____ (🥕) I jumped out of bed and brushed

my _____ (🐶) . I heard my _____ (🐋) .

_____ (🥕) _____ (🥕) I ran outside. A

_____ (🍍) _____ (🐋) stood on our lawn. It

was making a lot of noise. _____ (🥕)

It charged at the _____ (🐋) . There

were _____ (🐶) everywhere!

What's Next?

Fill in the next number for each pattern.

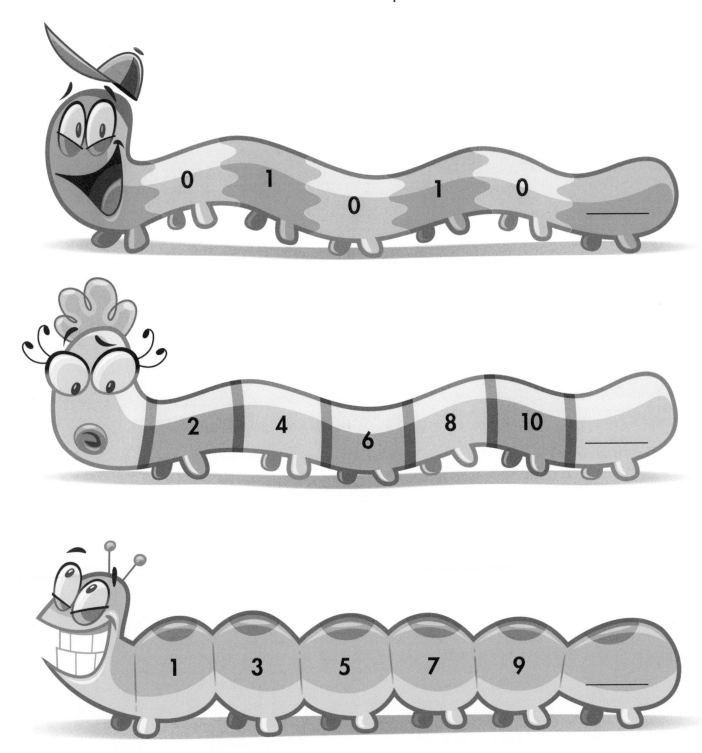

0   1   0   1   0   _____

2   4   6   8   10   _____

1   3   5   7   9   _____

Words can have patterns, too. Write words to match this pattern.

bake   make   _____   _____   _____

20   25   30   35   40   _____

3   6   9   12   15   _____

10   20   30   40   50   _____

A Colorful Garden

Color the **short o** words red.
Color the **long o** words yellow.

The word garden can be a noun and a verb.

How long did you _____ in the _____?

bzzz

frog

hot

cone

dot

box

soap

boat

toes

How to Clean a Dirty Dog

🐚	🧁	⚽	🍦
milk	soft	blow	bone
socks	rotten	rinse	yo-yo
soap	fuzzy	soak	goat
towels	good	poke	coat

Did your dog play in the mud? Is she dirty? Here

is how to clean her. Take a tub and fill it with

_____ _____ . Then

add a _____ . Put your dog in the tub.

_____ the dirt away. Dry her with _____

_____ . Then _____ your dog's

_____ . Now she is clean. She's a _____

puppy! Give her a _____ _____ .

Oh no! Is she back in the mud? Well, now you know just what to do.

53

Joining Words Together

A **conjunction** joins words or parts of sentences.
The words **and**, **but**, and **or** are conjunctions.

Add **and**, **but**, or **or** to finish each sentence.

I like baseball _____ soccer.

We need to hurry _____ we'll be late.

My sister takes piano lessons, _____ she can't play very well.

You could either take the bus to the store _____ you could ride your bike.

My three favorite colors are red, orange, _____ yellow.

I ate four hot dogs, _____ I'm still hungry.

Liar, Liar

🍌	🐋	🥕	🐶
moon	banana	wrestled	camera
North Pole	hippo	licked	sausage
zoo	gerbil	tickled	crocodile
ballpark	lollipop	juggled	giraffe

I know a man whose nose grows longer every time he lies. Once he

said that he saw a _____ 🐋 or a _____ 🐶 fly

to the _____ 🍌 . His nose grew longer. Then, he said his

_____ 🐋 _____ 🥕 a _____ 🐶 .

Next, he said that he went on vacation to the _____ 🍌 !

Now his nose was as long as a _____ 🐋 ! It reached all

the way to the _____ 🍌 ! So I

_____ 🥕 it. What! You don't

believe me? Are my pants on fire?

55

Slowly or Quickly?

An **adverb** tells how an action is done.

Circle the adverb in each sentence.
Then underline the action it describes.

The firefighter bravely dashed into the burning building.

Whoops! I accidentally spilled some water.

She nodded silently to her friend.

The turtle slowly crawled down the path.

Hold the glass vase carefully or it may break.

Fun at the Beach

🍕	⚽	🌊	🍦
dragon	carefully	dribble	backpacks
monster	loudly	squirt	teeth
crab	slowly	pinch	buckets
toilet	rudely	spread	boots
pirate	quickly	tickle	shells

Come with me to the beach. We can make a _____ out
🍕

of sand. Here's how. First, _____ _____
⚽ 🌊

wet sand into _____ . Then, _____ the
🍦 🌊

sand on the _____ . Do it _____ or it
🍕 ⚽

will _____ . Then, _____ pat down the
🌊 ⚽

sand. Use _____ to make the _____ . You
🍦 🍦

finished your sand art. WAIT! Is that

a giant wave?

Short or Long?

Draw a circle around each word with a **short u** sound.
Draw a rectangle around each word with a **long u** sound.

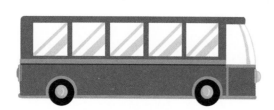

a blue bus

a huge truck

a glum duck

a cute bug

a funny mummy

a tube of glue

An Unusual Concert

🌶	🦆	🦔	🍅
flute	blue	run	mud
tuba	huge	jump	gum
trumpet	glum	cry	bugs
drum	cute	dance	buses
bugle	rude	laugh	slugs

Sue went to a concert. One player had a _____.
🌶

He played out of tune. Another player had a _____
🦆

_____ made of _____. A player with a
🌶   🍅

_____ tried to _____ on the stage. When
🌶   🦔

she played, _____ flew out of her instrument. At the
🍅

end, a singer sang a _____
🦆

song about a _____ unicorn
🦆

that couldn't _____.
🦔

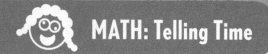

Monster Time

Write the correct time under each clock.

This is when Monster wakes up: _____

This is when Monster eats: _____

When the long hand points to the **12**, we say o'clock. So Monster goes to sleep at _____ o'clock. When does he wake up? _____ o'clock

This is when Monster plays ball: _____

This is when Monster goes to sleep: _____

What Does It Sound Like?

Some words sound like the things they describe.

Write a **sound word** for each picture.

| swish | achoo | tick-tock |
| toot | buzz | slurp |

_____ _____ _____

_____ _____ _____

Listen Carefully

🌶️	🌴	🦋	🐚
birds	purple	trickling	Crash!
bees	fat	buzzing	Splash!
trucks	striped	chirping	Shh!
kangaroos	hairy	howling	Vroom!

_____ Stop and listen. Can you hear the water
🐚

_____ in the stream? _____ Some
🦋   🐚

_____ _____ just jumped in! What
🌴   🌶️

about the _____? They are
🌶️

_____ in the _____
🦋   🌴

trees. Can you hear them? _____
🐚

What was that? A bunch of _____
🌴

_____ just came by!
🌶️

63

Picture This

When two **consonants** are together in a word, we often hear the sound of both letters.

Add two letters to finish each picture name.

___ ___ ooter

___ ___ apes

___ ___ ower

___ ___ oon

___ ___ um

___ ___ ee

Three Goats

⚽	👕	🐟	🧁
pretzels	grumpy	sniff	highway
slugs	green	tickle	circus
fleas	skinny	eat	truck
grapes	smelly	scratch	bathtub
snakes	fluffy	gobble	store

Once there were three _____ 👕 goats. They lived

on the side of a _____ 🧁 . There weren't any

_____ ⚽ to _____ 🐟 . But not far away

was a bridge to a _____ 🧁 . The goats crossed the bridge.

Under the bridge lived a _____ 👕 troll. "Go away or I

will jump up and _____ 🐟 you!" roared

the troll. "Come on up," the goats said. Then they

all shared a bowl of _____ ⚽ .

How Much?

The monsters each want to buy a lollipop. Write the amount of money each monster has. Then circle the monster with enough money to buy the treat.

23 cents

 1 cent

 5 cents

 10 cents

 25 cents

I have _____ cents.

Money can be written in different ways. 10 cents and 10¢ and ten cents all mean the same thing. Fill in the blanks.

50 cents or _____

or _____

I have _____ cents.

I have _____ cents.

Tell Me More!

Prepositions tell more about a noun or verb in a sentence.

Look at each picture. Add a preposition to finish each sentence.

in   **over**   **on**   **under**

The cat is sleeping

_____ the chair.

The dog is hiding

_____ the bed.

The goldfish is swimming

_____ the bowl.

The frog is jumping

_____ the rock.

Lost and Found

🥕	🐟	🍅	🦴
tooth	under	broken	toes
elephant	behind	smelly	socks
piano	on	sweet	crumbs
nose	beside	magic	ants
pickle	above	drippy	beans

Oh no! I lost my _____ . Where can it be? 🥕

Is it _____ the bed? No, but here are 🐟

my _____ _____ . Maybe 🍅 🦴

it's _____ the stairs. No, but I found a 🐟

_____ _____ . I wonder 🍅 🥕

if it's _____ the cereal box. No, I only 🐟

found some _____ . Here it is! It was 🦴

_____ my _____ ! 🐟 🥕

69

Word Salad

Read each word below. If the word starts with a **hard c** sound, like **carrot**, write the word next to the carrot. If the word starts with a **soft c** sound, like **celery**, write the word next to the celery.

cereal   car   cookies

candle   city   circle

Hard c Words

_____

_____

_____

Soft c Words

_____

_____

_____

Come to the Circus!

🍌	🦔	🍍	🧁
city	bouncy	cook	crayons
car	fancy	curl up	cookies
castle	crispy	bounce	combs
cow	cute	cough	cakes
cloud	cool	dance	mice

The circus is in town! Step inside the big _____ . See the
🍌

_____ magic show. Watch _____ acrobats
🦔 🦔

tumble and _____ across the _____ .
🍍 🍌

Laugh at the _____ clowns with _____ in
🦔 🧁

their hair. Buy popcorn and _____ . Clap for the seals
🧁

when they _____ . Gasp when the lion tamer
🍍

puts _____ in the lion's mouth! There
🧁

is so much for you to see and do at the circus!

71

It's a Date!

The monsters have a busy summer.
Use the calendar to answer the questions.

JULY

SUNDAY	MONDAY	TUESDAY	WEDNESDAY	THURSDAY	FRIDAY	SATURDAY
		1	2	3	4	5
6	7	8	9	10	11	12
13	14	15	16	17	18	19
20	21	22	23	24	25	26
27	28	29	30	31		

 There are 12 months in the year. Write the month when you were born.

_____

The monsters want to see fireworks. What day of the

week is the Fourth of July? _____

Every Friday, the monsters go swimming. How many times

will they go swimming in July? _____

The monsters are going to a picnic on July 28. Circle

the date on the calendar.

The monsters have a party on the second Saturday of July.

What is the date? _____

The monsters are going to the beach on the last

day of July. What day is that? _____

Alike but Different

Homophones are words that sound alike but are not spelled the same.

Read each sentence.
Circle the word with the correct spelling.

I had a (grate / great) time on my trip.

I went to (sea / see) the (sea / see).

The (sun / son) was shining.

I saw a (pair / pear) of dolphins.

Then (ate / eight) fish swam by.

The Tale of the Tail

🐶	🐟	🌴	🍕
silly	caterpillar	fluffy	kiss
brave	rabbit	hairy	cook
strong	dinosaur	pink	sit on
grumpy	crocodile	plump	sniff
rude	squirrel	sharp	lick

One night a _____ knight was riding his
🐶

_____ . The knight was as hungry as
🐟

a _____ . He ate eight eggs and a pair of
🐟

_____ pears. Then he saw
🌴

a _____ tail disappear behind a tree.
🌴

The knight tried to _____ it. Yikes! It
🍕

belonged to a _____ bear. The bear tried to
🐶

_____ the knight! The knight dashed away.
🍕

75

Sentence Enders

Add end marks to the story. Use a **period** (.),
question mark (?), or an **exclamation point** (!).

Hooray _____   Today is my birthday _____

Six kids are coming to my party _____

I'm having chocolate cake and ice cream _____

Can I blow out all the candles _____

I hope my wish comes true _____

Can you guess what I wished for _____

Wow _____   I got a new puppy _____

Birthday wishes can come true _____

Space Camp

🦆	🦔	🐋	🍦
peanut butter	exploded	silly	Hooray!
rocks	burped	sticky	Blast off!
cheese	froze	fuzzy	Sardines!
toenails	rolled over	round	Oh no!

Dear Mom and Dad,

Camp is fun! Today we made a _____ rocket out of
🐋

cardboard and _____ . Then we _____
🦆   🦔

it. Then our rocket was as _____ as a gerbil. Someone
🐋

_____ the rocket. "_____" we yelled.
🦔   🍦

Now our rocket looked like _____ . Do you think we're
🦆

ready to fly to the _____ moon?
🐋

_____
🍦

Love, Jayden

77

Pizza Party!

The monsters are having a pizza party.
Cross out the number of pizza slices that each monster ate.

I ate 1 slice of pizza.

I ate 2 slices of pizza.

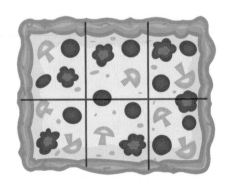

One half of a pizza plus one half of a pizza equals one whole pizza!

I ate 3 slices of pizza.

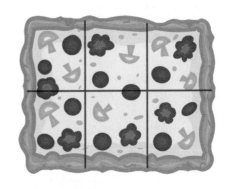

I ate 4 slices of pizza. That's half the pizza!

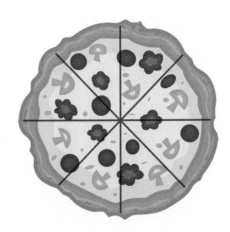

Rhyme Time

Rhyming words end with the same sound.

Match each animal to the object that rhymes with its name.

Fashion Nonsense

👕	🍕	🐶	🧁
hairy	marching	fluffy	basketball
clever	dancing	purple	car
fancy	licking	polka-dot	lollipop
smelly	snoring	rubber	pickle

Guess what I saw at the fashion show?

a _____ pig in a _____
   👕   🐶

wig _____ on a _____
       🍕   🧁

a _____ goat in a _____
   👕   🐶

coat _____ by a _____
        🍕   🧁

a _____ fox with _____
   👕   🐶

socks _____ a _____
         🍕   🧁

Cut It Out!

A **contraction** is a shortened way to write two words. The letter or letters left out are replaced by an apostrophe (').

Write the contraction for each word pair.

I am _____   he is _____

they are _____   we are _____

you will _____   let us _____

Write the word pair for each contraction.

aren't _____   there's _____

it's _____   hasn't _____

doesn't _____   won't _____

Table Manners

🍍	🦴	🦋	🍉
greasy	eyes	burp	book
silly	boogers	sing	salad
drippy	carrots	slurp	shirt
hot	elbows	chomp	hamster

When you're a dinner guest, you need good table manners.

1. It isn't polite to _____ when people
🦋

are talking.

2. You shouldn't _____ holding
🦋

a _____ .
🍉

3. When you're eating _____
🍍

_____ , don't _____ .
🦴 🦋

4. Let's keep our _____ _____ off
🍍 🦴

our _____ .
🍉

Who Am I?

You can add **er** and **est** to an adjective to compare things.
Add **er** when you are comparing two things.
Add **est** when you are comparing three or more things.

Add an adjective to finish each sentence.

short   **shorter**   **shortest**

I am the _____ boy in my class.

tall   **taller**   **tallest**

But I am _____ than my sister.

old   **older**   **oldest**

My brother is _____ than me.

tall   **taller**   **tallest**

My brother is the _____ kid in our family.

Come to the Fair!

🍕	👕	🦆	🐋
taller	tomato	quickest	robots
longer	pumpkin	smallest	toenails
slower	teacup	smartest	snails
sadder	spider	loudest	grasshoppers

The fair is open! You can ride a whirly _____ .
                                                    👕

It is _____ than a _____ .
              🍕   👕

You can see _____ race. Which one will be the
                    🐋

_____ of them all? The judges will pick the
        🦆

_____ _____ . Second
        🦆   👕

place gets a big bag of _____ .
                                🐋

They are _____ than a
                  🍕

_____ . Hungry? Time for
        👕

some fried _____ .
                    🐋

85

Caterpillar Sentences

You can add **s**, **ed**, or **ing** to a verb, or action word.

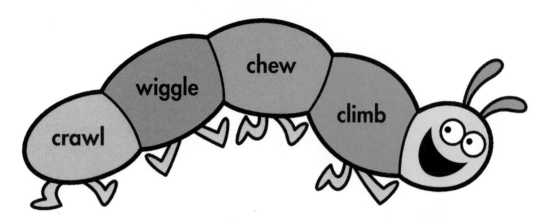

Choose a word from the caterpillar. Add **s**. Use your new word to write a sentence about the caterpillar.

_____

_____

Choose another word from the caterpillar. Add **ed**. Use your new word to write a sentence about the caterpillar.

_____

_____

Choose a third word from the caterpillar. Add **ing**. Use your new word to write a sentence about the caterpillar.

_____

_____

Summer Fun

🍫	⚽	🐚	🦆
laughing	painted	spider	grumpy
burping	wrestled	nose	silly
scratching	cooked	bike	fuzzy
jumping	melted	fish	striped

Dear Diary,

Yesterday was fun. In the morning, I _____ my
⚽
toys. Then I rode my _____ with my brother. For
🐚
lunch, we _____ a _____ . Then we
⚽   🐚

watched a _____ movie about a _____ . It
🦆   🐚

_____ a _____ crocodile! Today
⚽   🦆

is very hot. I can hear my brother _____ .
🍫

He is _____ in the pool. I'm going to
🍫

join him!

87

Riddle Me This

When two **consonants** are together in a word, we often hear the sound of both letters.

Add two letters to answer each riddle.

What's green and hops? ___ ___ og

What helps you tell time? ___ ___ ock

What has eight legs and spins a web? ___ ___ ider

What has wheels and wings? ___ ___ ane

What twinkles in the sky at night? ___ ___ ar

Quiz Time

🐋	🌶️	👕	🍅
spit	chipmunks	drawing	in my hat
snort	bubbles	twisting	on the grass
chuckle	bricks	cleaning	in the tub
swim	plums	juggling	on the plane

Are you a funny kid? Take this quiz and find out!

☐ I like to _____ 🐋 while _____ 👕

_____ 🌶️ .

☐ I like to _____ 🐋 while _____ 👕

_____ 🍅 .

☐ I like to _____ 🐋 _____ 🍅 .

☐ I like to _____ 🐋 while

_____ 👕 _____ 🌶️ .

Did you check all the answers? Then you are **very** funny!

Picture Puzzles

Compound words are two or more words that join together to make a new word.

Write a compound word for each pair of pictures.

_____ + _____ = _____

Draw a picture of one of the compound words.

A Mystery

🦔	🦋	🍍
footprints	playground	ladybug
raincoats	bedroom	flagpole
rattlesnakes	hallway	sweatshirt
bookshelves	doghouse	backpack

Someone broke my best flowerpot. It was in the shape of a

_____ 🍍 . But who did it? I looked for clues. I found three

_____ 🦔 in the garden. They led to a _____ 🍍

in the _____ 🦋 . Nearby was a _____ 🍍 and a

pair of _____ 🦔 . Could these things be clues, too? Nearby

was my sister's _____ 🍍 . I saw that her _____ 🦔

were covered in dirt. Then my sister walked in. She

handed me two _____ 🦔 . "Sorry, I broke

your flowerpot," she said. Mystery solved!

91

PHONICS: Short Vowel a/Long Vowel a

A Is for Animal

Read each word pair.
Draw a circle around the words with the **short a** sound.
Draw a rectangle around the words with the **long a** sound.

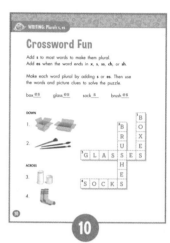

snake | bat
map | ape
skates | lamb
plane | cat
cap | whale
cake | rabbit

6

VOCABULARY: Prefixes

Picture This!

A **prefix** is a word part added to the beginning of a word.
It changes the meaning of the word.
Underline the **prefix** in each sentence. Then draw a picture about the sentence.

The runner's shoelace is untied.

> Pictures will vary.

Return the book to the library.

The magician made the rabbit disappear.

The clown is wearing mismatched socks.

8

WRITING: Plurals s, es

Crossword Fun

Add **s** to most words to make them plural.
Add **es** when the word ends in **x, s, ss, ch,** or **sh**.

Make each word plural by adding **s** or **es**. Then use the words and picture clues to solve the puzzle.

box **es**   glass **es**   sock **s**   brush **es**

DOWN
1.
2.

ACROSS
3.
4.

BOXES
BRUSHES
GLASSES
SOCKS

10

MATH: Even and Odd Numbers

Monster Toes

Count each monster's toes. Draw a circle around the monsters with an even number of toes.
Draw a rectangle around the monsters with an odd number of toes.

> Plural means more than one of something.

Number of toes: 6
Number of toes: 8
Number of toes: 9
Number of toes: 10
Number of toes: 5
Number of toes: 7

Toes is the plural for __toe__.
Feet is the plural for __foot__.

12   13

12–13

VOCABULARY: Sensory Words

Find the Words

Words that describe things using our five senses are called **sensory words**. The five senses are **sight, sound, touch, smell,** and **taste**.

Find the 10 sensory words in the word search.

shiny   bumpy   squeaky   smooth   wrinkled
spicy   ringing   salty   buzzing   fishy

14

PHONICS: Short Vowel e/Long Vowel e

Animal Matchup

What words have a **short e** sound?
Draw a line from those words to the **hen**.

What words have a **long e** sound?
Draw a line from those words to the **seal**.

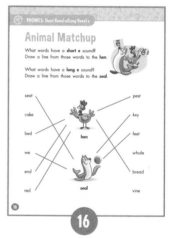

seat   pest
cake   key
bed   feet
we   hen   whale
end   bread
red   seal   vine

16

MATH: Basic Shapes

Shape Town

Welcome to Shape Town!
How many of these shapes can you find?

Trace the shapes found in the picture.

> This word circle can be both a noun and a verb.

18   19

18–19

WRITING: Nouns

Not a Noun

A **noun** is a naming word.
A person, place, or thing is a noun.
Circle the word in each box that is not a **noun**.

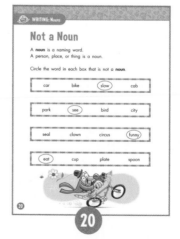

car | bike | (slow) | cab
park | (see) | bird | city
seal | clown | circus | (funny)
(eat) | cup | plate | spoon

20

PHONICS: Short Vowel i/Long Vowel i

Piggy Bank Fun

Write each word on the correct bank.

six   kind   pig   five
pie   fish   dime   pink

Long i Sounds
pie
kind
dime
five

Short i Sounds
six
fish
pig
pink

22

MATH: Addition and Subtraction

Color By Number

Color in each space that equals 5. What do you see?

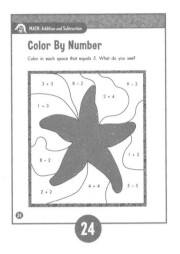

3 + 3	8 – 2	9 – 3
1 + 3		2 + 4
8 – 2		1 + 2
2 + 2	4 + 4	5 – 5

24

Tic-Tac-Toe Math

Draw a circle around the three problems with matching answers in each square. Look across, down, and diagonally.

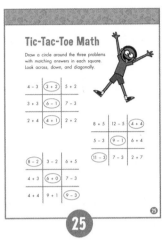

4 – 3	3 + 2	5 + 2
3 + 3	6 – 1	4 + 1
2 + 4	4 + 1	2 + 2

8 + 5	12 – 5	4 + 4
5 – 3	9 – 1	6 + 4
11 – 3	7 – 3	2 + 7

8 – 2	3 – 2	6 + 5
4 + 3	6 + 0	7 – 3
4 + 4	9 + 1	9 – 3

25

WRITING: Verbs

Tough Tongue Twisters

A **verb** is an action word. Every sentence has a verb.

Circle the verb in each tongue twister.

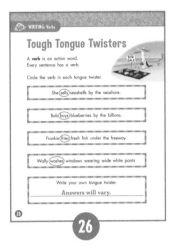

She sells seashells by the seashore.

Bob buys blueberries by the billions.

Frankie fries fresh fish under the freeway.

Wally washes windows wearing wide white pants.

Write your own tongue twister.
Answers will vary.

26

VOCABULARY: Verbs

A Wet Trip

Add a **verb** to finish each sentence.

jogged   raced   skipped   walked

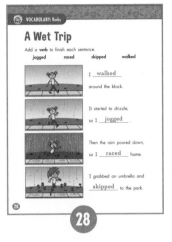

I **walked** around the block.

It started to drizzle, so I **jogged**.

Then the rain poured down, so I **raced** home.

I grabbed an umbrella and **skipped** to the park.

28

MATH: Writing Number Sentences

Tasty Treats

Count the treats in each group.
Write the numbers in the boxes.
Then write the answer to the problem in the last box.

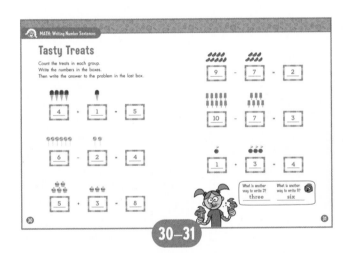

4 + 1 = 5

6 – 2 = 4

5 + 3 = 8

9 – 7 = 2

10 – 7 = 3

1 + 3 = 4

What is another way to write 3? **three**

What is another way to write 6? **six**

30–31

PHONICS: Food's

Word Magic

Presto the Magician can change a cub into a cube. How? He adds **e**.
Help Presto change the words below. Add **e** to finish each word. Then draw a picture of the new word.

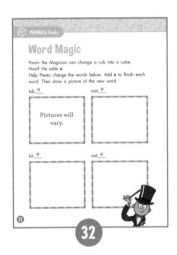

tub**e**   can**e**

Pictures will vary.

kit**e**   not**e**

32

VOCABULARY: Word Categories

Sort It Out!

This room is a mess! Put the words in the correct category.

ball   kite   pizza
cap   apple   game
sock   shirt   carrot

Clothes Words	Food Words	Toy Words
sock	apple	ball
shirt	pizza	kite
cap	carrot	game

34

WRITING: Adjectives

Which Way to the Picnic?

An **adjective** is a word that describes something.

The ants are going to a picnic.
Help them get there by following the path of adjectives.

36

PHONICS: Digraphs

Fill In the Blanks

When two or more consonants are together in a word, they sometimes make a new sound.

Circle the letters to make a word that matches the picture. Then write the letters in the blanks to complete each word.

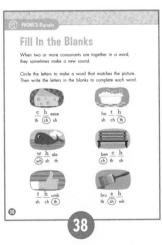

ch eese   th **ch** sh

ba **th**   sh ch **th**

wh ale   **wh** sh th

ben **ch**   **ch** th sh

th umb   sh ch **th**

bru **sh**   th **sh** wh

38

VOCABULARY: Adjectives

Laugh It Up!

Add an adjective to finish each sentence.

funny   hilarious   ridiculous   clever

I heard a **clever** joke. It made me think.

I read a **funny** book. I giggled all the way through.

I saw a **hilarious** movie. I never laughed so hard.

My sister played a **ridiculous** prank on me. NOT funny!

40

Fun at the Pool

A **pronoun** takes the place of a noun.

Add a pronoun to finish each sentence.

I   you   her
it   we   me

__I__ am going to the pool.

My friend is going with __me__.

She is bringing __her__ float.

__It__ is big and green.

__We__ will have fun!

Do __you__ want to come?

42

Who Can Ride?

These creatures want to go on a ride. Use the tickets to measure each creature and write down your answers. Circle the creature who is tall enough to ride.

Write three plural nouns from the picture.
Answers will vary.

__4__ __3__ __8__ __5__

44—45

Gee, You're Great!

Read each word. If the word starts with a **hard g** sound, like **gorilla**, write the word next to the **gorilla**. If the word starts with a **soft g** sound, like **giraffe**, write the word next to the **giraffe**.

gentle   gym   goat
germ   garden   game

Hard g Words
goat
garden
game

Soft g Words
gentle
gym
germ

46

Riddle Me This

What animal wears a coat in the winter and pants in the summer?

Find the answer to the riddle. Color in the lowercase letters in the picture.

The animal is a __dog__.

48

What's Next?

Fill in the next number for each pattern.

Words can have patterns, too. Write words to match this pattern.
bake make **Answers will vary.**

0 1 0 1 0 __1__

2 4 6 8 10 __12__

3 6 9 12 15 __18__

1 3 5 7 9 __11__

20 25 30 35 40 __45__

10 20 30 40 50 __60__

50—51

A Colorful Garden

Color the **short o** words red.
Color the **long o** words yellow.

The word garden can be a noun and a verb.

How long did you __garden__ in the __garden__?

frog — red
hot — red
cone — yellow
dot — red
box — red
soap — yellow
boat — yellow
toes — yellow

52

Joining Words Together

A **conjunction** joins words or parts of sentences. The words **and**, **but**, and **or** are conjunctions.

Add **and**, **but**, or **or** to finish each sentence.

I like baseball __and__ soccer.

We need to hurry __or__ we'll be late.

My sister takes piano lessons, __but__ she can't play very well.

You could either take the bus to the store __or__ you could ride your bike.

My three favorite colors are red, orange, __and__ yellow.

I ate four hot dogs, __but__ I'm still hungry.

54

Slowly or Quickly?

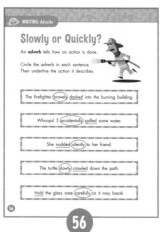

An **adverb** tells how an action is done.

Circle the adverb in each sentence. Then underline the action it describes.

The firefighter (bravely) <u>dashed</u> into the burning building.

Whoops! I (accidentally) <u>spilled</u> some water.

She <u>nodded</u> (silently) to her friend.

The turtle (slowly) <u>crawled</u> down the path.

Hold the glass vase (carefully) or it may break.

56

94

Short or Long?

Draw a circle around each word with a **short u** sound.
Draw a rectangle around each word with a **long u** sound.

a blue bus   a huge truck

a glum duck   a cute bug

a funny mummy   a tube of glue

58

Monster Time

Write the correct time under each clock.

> When the long hand points to the 12, we say o'clock. So Monster goes to sleep at __8__ o'clock. When does he wake up? __7__ o'clock.

This is when Monster wakes up: ___7:00___

This is when Monster plays ball: ___2:15___

This is when Monster eats: ___9:30___

This is when Monster goes to sleep: ___8:00___

60–61

What Does It Sound Like?

Some words sound like the things they describe.

Write a **sound word** for each picture.

swish   achoo   tick-tock
toot   buzz   slurp

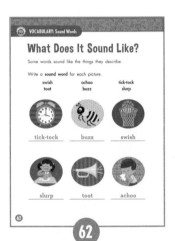

tick-tock   buzz   swish

slurp   toot   achoo

62

Picture This

When two **consonants** are together in a word, we often hear the sound of both letters.

Add two letters to finish each picture name.

s_c_ ooter   g_r_ apes

f_l_ ower   s_p_ oon

d_r_ um   t_r_ ee

64

How Much?

The monsters each want to buy a lollipop. Write the amount of money each monster has. Then circle the monster with enough money to buy the treat.

23 cent

> Money can be written in different ways. 10 cents and 10¢ and ten cents all mean the same thing. Fill in the blanks.
> 50 cents or __50¢__ or __fifty cents__

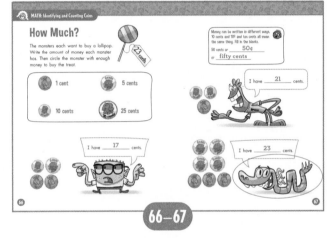

1 cent   5 cents
10 cents   25 cents

I have __21__ cents.

I have __17__ cents.

I have __23__ cents.

66–67

Tell Me More!

Prepositions tell more about a noun or verb in a sentence.

Look at each picture. Add a preposition to finish each sentence.

in   over   on   under

The cat is sleeping ___on___ the chair.

The dog is hiding ___under___ the bed.

The goldfish is swimming ___in___ the bowl.

The frog is jumping ___over___ the rock.

68

Word Salad

Read each word below. If the word starts with a **hard c** sound, like **carrot**, write the word next to the carrot. If the word starts with a **soft c** sound, like **celery**, write the word next to the celery.

cereal   car   cookies
candle   city   circle

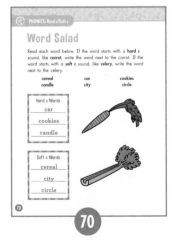

Hard c Words
car
cookies
candle

Soft c Words
cereal
city
circle

70

It's a Date!

The monsters have a busy summer. Use the calendar to answer the questions.

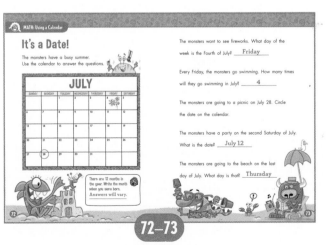

JULY

SUNDAY	MONDAY	TUESDAY	WEDNESDAY	THURSDAY	FRIDAY	SATURDAY
				1	2	3
4	5	6	7	8	9	10
11	12	13	14	15	16	17
18	19	20	21	22	23	24
25	26	27	28	29	30	31

> There are 12 months in the year. Write the month when you were born. Answers will vary.

The monsters want to see fireworks. What day of the week is the Fourth of July? ___Friday___

Every Friday, the monsters go swimming. How many times will they go swimming in July? ___4___

The monsters are going to a picnic on July 28. Circle the date on the calendar.

The monsters have a party on the second Saturday of July. What is the date? ___July 12___

The monsters are going to the beach on the last day of July. What day is that? ___Thursday___

72–73

95

VOCABULARY: Homophones

Alike but Different

Homophones are words that sound alike but are not spelled the same.

Read each sentence.
Circle the word with the correct spelling.

I had a (grate / (great)) time on my trip.

I went to (sea / (see)) the (sea) / see).

The ((sun) / son) was shining.

I saw a ((pair) / pear) of dolphins.

Then (ate / (eight)) fish swam by.

74

WRITING: End Punctuation

Sentence Enders

Add end marks to the story. Use a **period** (.), **question mark** (?), or an **exclamation point** (!).

Hooray __!__ Today is my birthday __.__

Six kids are coming to my party __.__

I'm having chocolate cake and ice cream __.__

Can I blow out all the candles __?__

I hope my wish comes true __.__

Can you guess what I wished for __?__

Wow __!__ I got a new puppy __.__

Birthday wishes can come true __.__

76

MATH: Fractions

Pizza Party!

The monsters are having a pizza party.
Cross out the number of pizza slices that each monster ate.

One half of a pizza plus one half of a pizza equals one whole pizza!

I ate 1 slice of pizza.

I ate 3 slices of pizza.

I ate 2 slices of pizza.

I ate 4 slices of pizza. That's half the pizza!

78–79

VOCABULARY: Rhyming Words

Rhyme Time

Rhyming words end with the same sound.

Match each animal to the object that rhymes with its name.

80

WRITING: Contractions

Cut It Out!

A **contraction** is a shortened way to write two words. The letter or letters left out are replaced by an apostrophe (').

Write the contraction for each word pair.

I am __I'm__   he is __he's__

they are __they're__   we are __we're__

you will __you'll__   let us __let's__

Write the word pair for each contraction.

aren't __are not__   there's __there is__

it's __it is__   hasn't __has not__

doesn't __does not__   won't __will not__

82

VOCABULARY: Comparative Words er, est

Who Am I?

You can add **er** and **est** to an adjective to compare things.
Add **er** when you are comparing two things.
Add **est** when you are comparing three or more things.

Add an adjective to finish each sentence.

short   shorter   shortest
I am the __shortest__ boy in my class.

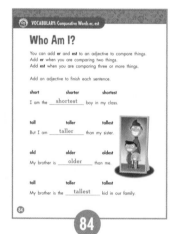

tall   taller   tallest
But I am __taller__ than my sister.

old   older   oldest
My brother is __older__ than me.

tall   taller   tallest
My brother is the __tallest__ kid in our family.

84

WRITING: Inflectional Endings s, ed, ing

Caterpillar Sentences

You can add **s**, **ed**, or **ing** to a verb, or action word.

crawl, wiggle, chew, climb

Choose a word from the caterpillar. Add **s**. Use your new word to write a sentence about the caterpillar.
__Words will vary.__
__Sentences will vary.__

Choose another word from the caterpillar. Add **ed**. Use your new word to write a sentence about the caterpillar.
__Words will vary.__
__Sentences will vary.__

Choose a third word from the caterpillar. Add **ing**. Use your new word to write a sentence about the caterpillar.
__Words will vary.__
__Sentences will vary.__

86

PHONICS: Blends

Riddle Me This

When two **consonants** are together in a word, we often hear the sound of both letters.

Add two letters to answer each riddle.

What's green and hops? __f__ __r__ og

What helps you tell time? __c__ __l__ ock

What has eight legs and spins a web? __s__ __p__ ider

What has wheels and wings? __p__ __l__ ane

What twinkles in the sky at night? __s__ __t__ ar

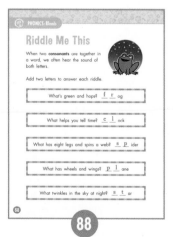

88

VOCABULARY: Compound Words

Picture Puzzles

Compound words are two or more words that join together to make a new word.

Write a compound word for each pair of pictures.

+ = __pancake__

+ = __sunflower__

+ = __butterfly__

Draw a picture of one of the compound words.

__Pictures will vary.__

90